AF439842

Contents

Introduction

A hedge or hedgerow is a line of closely spaced shrubs and sometimes trees, planted and trained to form a barrier or to mark the boundary of an area, such as between neighbouring properties. Hedges used to separate a road from adjoining fields or one field from another, and of sufficient age to incorporate larger trees, are known as hedgerows. Often they serve as windbreaks to improve conditions for the adjacent crops, as in bocage country. When clipped and maintained, hedges are also a simple form of topiary.

Hedges are ideal for security and privacy and provide thick yet attractive screening. They can also be used as backgrounds to other garden plants and features or simply be enjoyed in their own right. A neat hedge combined with a classic garden arch makes an attractive and practical garden feature.

A hedging plant should be chosen for its leaf size, natural growth habit or texture if sculpturing or pruning is to be employed. Size wise, hedges range from tall (Yew) to small edging box or lavender types. It is important to take into account local climate conditions, as some plants such as Yew require quite formal treatment, while others such as Hawthorn require much more informal attention.

Large plants such as Laurel are generally planted as a single row, while smaller types such as Blackthorn, Beech or Hawthorn are planted in staggered row to encourage greater density. When pruning or clipping your hedge, you should make the hedge narrower at the top than the bottom. This allows light to fall across all parts of the hedge, encouraging leaf growth even at ground level where it may otherwise be too dark for successful growth and lower branches will become quite bare and die away. This review will give you detailed information about hedge garden.

What Are Hedges?

Hedges are living boundaries made by planting a row of trees, and later cutting them in a special way and 'laying' the stems to create a hedge a barrier that can last for thousands of years if maintained well. They're more of a lowland phenomenon with dry stone walls often being used in higher areas such as the Yorkshire Moors and Dales.

Different styles of hedgelaying emerged from different parts of the country. The prevalent style is Midland, in which the stems are laid at angle, giving the hedges height and making them a barrier for cattle. In the South-West, where the livestock is predominantly sheep, the stem is cut and laid horizontally, which doesn't give as much height.

There are several other styles, and in Devon and Cornwall there are often hedge-banks, partly because poor soil prevents the growth of vigorous hedges, and partly because sites are exposed. They're hard work, but were built centuries ago, to mark out very small holdings.

What To Plant In a Hedge Garden

Most trees and shrubs have potential to make hedges. More information on suitable species can be found on our selecting plants for hedging page.

Hedging plants are often supplied as bare-root specimens, which are usually inexpensive. However, pot-grown plants are equally suitable but cost a little more. Evergreens, especially, are often sold as root-wrapped, where the roots are in a soil ball contained by a fabric casing. This wrapping must be removed, if it is of synthetic fibre, but natural fibre wrappings are sometimes left on. Removal of wrapping is still recommended, though.

Small hedge plants are often called whips and are about 60cm (2ft) high. They are very cheap and are easy to establish. Larger plants need more care and are more expensive. It is best to plant whips closely as they not only form a thick hedge, but compete with each other and so reduce the amount of trimming required.

When To Plant a Hedge

- Evergreen and semi-evergreen hedges: Early autumn is ideal for hedging plants such as box, privet (semi-evergreen) and yew. However, they can be planted at any time from late autumn until late winter.
- Deciduous hedges: Plant beech, hawthorn and hornbeam any time from leaf fall. This is typically from mid-autumn until late winter

In all cases, planting is best delayed until the soil can be worked easily, especially if the ground is frozen or waterlogged. If there is a delay in planting, keep the plants in a frost-free shed and cover their roots with moist straw, paper or potting compost and plastic sheet. This will prevent them drying out. Alternatively, they can be temporarily planted very close together in a trench, with their roots covered in at least 20cm (8in) of soil (this is called heeling-in).

How To Plant a Hedge

Planting and caring for a new hedge is very similar to that for any new tree or shrub. Good soil preparation beforehand will give your hedge the best start in life.

- Soil preparation

Prepare the ground by digging over a strip 60-90cm (2-3ft) wide and one spit (or spade blade) deep

If a herbicide (weedkiller) has not been used beforehand, remove all weeds. Soils that become waterlogged in winter may require a permanent drainage system. Alternatively, form the soil into a ridge about 15-20cm (6-8in) high and 50-70cm (20-28in) across to plant into. Do not add organic matter to the bottom of the trench as it decomposes causing the shrub to sink.

- Species

Get hedge plants from a specialist nursery. The important thing is that the plants are native species, which will be most useful to wildlife; but also that they're grown in the UK, from UK stock. Then genetically, plants will be suited to UK conditions and wildlife, they don't have to be transported as far, and you won't be importing any plant diseases or pests. Suppliers aren't obliged to tell you where plants come from, so you'll need to ask; or go to a nursery that you know is growing the plants, rather than just re-selling. Do a bit of research to find them.

Hawthorn tends to be the main hedge species sold, but you can also choose plants to attract particular wildlife species – hazelnuts for dormice, for example; or species that flower early, to provide nectar for bees when there might not be much else around – cherry plums can flower in February. You can also plant species to provide food, like damson or plum.

For smallholders wanting stock-proof hedges, hawthorn grows quickly and has thorns, and blackthorn is good because it suckers, which thickens the base of the hedge (less useful in urban settings as you could get blackthorn suckers coming up all over your lawn).

Roses are good too – they can't be laid, but provide beauty with their flowers, and can fill in gaps and add bulk to the hedge. Field maple is a classic hedge species; plus there's spindle for calcareous soil, and dogwood or willow for wetter areas. But you can use almost any species for hedging.

- Planting

First prepare the area you're going to plant, by clearing it of grass and weeds (which will take all the nutrients from new hedge plants). Make a strip up to a metre wide, and try to keep it as weed-free as possible. Planting takes place in winter (as does laying), when the plants are dormant. Plant five plants per metre, typically in a double, staggered row – with around 50cm between the rows, although this can vary depending on how much space you have.

Ideally position boundary hedges so they are set back a little way (e.g. 90cm/3ft) from the boundary line. This will allow the hedge to fill out before it becomes an issue with overhanging the pavement or a neighbour's property. Within the row planting distances vary from 30-60cm (1-2ft), depending on the plants' final size, the size of hedge required and plant vigour. For hedges thicker than 90cm (3ft), plant a staggered double row 45cm (18in) apart, with plants 90cm (3ft) apart

Trim back damaged roots to healthy growth with sharp knife or old pair of secateurs. Spread out the roots, ensuring the planting depth is correct. The point where the roots flare out from the stem should be level with the surrounding soil; on container-grown plants, scrape away the compost from the top of the root ball to reveal this point .

On sandy or heavy clay soils, mix organic matter, such as garden compost or a proprietary tree and shrub planting mix, with the soil dug out from the hole to backfill. Alternatively, spread over the soil surface and mix into the top 25cm (10in) of soil with a fork (forking in).Work soil between the roots, firm plants in so that soil is in close contact with the roots. Water if the soil is dry Mulch to a depth of 7.5cm (3in) after planting to prevent weeds

- Laying

Before laying your hedge, you need to let it grow to around 2 metres tall, which might take 3-5 years. Once it's laid, you can keep it in shape by trimming it, and then lay it again after maybe ten years. You can reckon on laying around 10-20 metres of hedge per day, depending on the hedge's condition. Stems are cut almost all the way through to lay them.

Laying a new hedge is much easier than renovating an old hedge. With an old hedge, you'll probably need a chainsaw, as the stems can be quite thick. With a new hedge, the stems will be much thinner and you'll only need a billhook or a small axe or pruning saw. You'll also need a slasher for pulling out brambles and other undergrowth, plus a mallet for Midland syle (and sometimes for Devon or Dorset style), for hammering in the stakes. You can use secateurs to prune side shoots and thorny twigs – but it's a medieval skill, so it's not high-tech.

The stems are cut diagonally almost all the way through as they're laid. It's quite surprising the first time you see it – it looks as though the hedge will die. But it doesn't. Smallholders might do a portion of their hedges each year, rather than trying to do it all at the same time – less drastic and more fun. Plus if you use a contractor, it's best to spread the cost over several years.

Laying a neglected hedge that's been left to grow for 30-40 years. Much more difficult, needs a chainsaw as well as a billhook.

Midland style - stems are laid at a 45 degree angle, often against vertical willow stakes (which themselves take root), tied in with horizontals to make a framework. This makes a strong, tall barrier for cattle. Hedges can be stock-proof immediately after laying, but it depends on the determination and strength of the stock (or if they're goats, anything could happen). You can plant a hedge next to a fence, and as long as you maintain the hedge, it will remain stock-proof long after the fence has gone.

If hedges aren't managed and laid, the plants grow up and out, and you end up with a line of small trees – which is fine if that's what you want – but it won't be stock-proof. But you can leave standard trees to grow out of the hedge (any species), at least 20 metres apart; but remember that really big trees will shade and stunt the growth of the hedge around them.

You can plant a hedge around your urban garden, rather than fence panels or walls (including possibly a 'fedge' – a cross between a fence and a hedge, made of living willow). The benefits mentioned above apply, as well as the fact that hedges are baffles rather than impervious windbreaks, and so they don't get blown over, as fence panels sometimes do. But it's not an immediate fix. Some species grow faster than others, but it still takes time to grow. But if you have an old fence that will need to be replaced, you could plant a hedge next to it, and by the time the fence dies, the hedge will be there to take its place.

- Aftercare

Ensure plants are well-watered during dry spells for the next two years . Top-dress annually with a general-purpose fertiliser, such as Growmore at 70g per sq m (2oz per sq yd), and re-apply mulch as required. Keep the hedge and 45cm (18in) on each side weed-free

- Problems

Hedges might take three to seven years to attain their desired size. You can buy semi-mature hedges which, although costly, will give an instant hedge. Semi-mature plants require extra care in planting and watering. Hedges might need shelter in their initial years on exposed sites. Hedges, like other trees and shrubs, are vulnerable to establishment problems.

Hooper's Rule states that you can tell the age of a hedge by the number of different species in a 30-yard length (excluding ivy) – each species representing a century. There are major exceptions to this rule, because after the enclosures of common land, landowners often planted hedges with almost all hawthorn, because the thorns kept the commoners out. Also, new hedges are often planted with a mix of different species.

There are ancient hedges scattered across the country – often where agricultural land is poor and there hasn't been intensive farming. Exmoor is a good example, where there are a number of very old hedges. There are still Anglo-Saxon hedges alive and well in the UK, which is the epicentre of hedges – mainly because of the complicated history of enclosures. After WW2, the growth in industrial agriculture meant that thousands of miles of hedges were removed – although there's been a revival in recent years

Edge Laying

If hedges are not maintained and trimmed regularly, gaps tend to form at the base over many years. In essence, hedgelaying consists of cutting most of the way through the stem of each plant near the base, bending it over and interweaving or pleaching it between wooden stakes. This also encourages new growth from the base of each plant. Originally, the main purpose of hedgelaying was to ensure the hedge remained stock-proof. Some side branches were also removed and used as firewood.

The maintenance and laying of hedges to form an impenetrable barrier for farm animals is a skilled art. In Britain there are many local hedgelaying traditions, each with a distinct style. Hedges are still being laid today not only for aesthetic and functional purposes but also for their ecological role in helping wildlife and protecting against soil erosion.

Hedge Trimming

 An alternative to hedge laying is trimming using a tractor-mounted flail cutter or circular saw, or a hedge trimmer. The height of the cutting can be increased a little every year. Trimming a hedge helps to promote bushy growth. If a flail cutter is used, then the flail must be kept sharp to ensure that the cutting is effective on the hedge.

The disadvantage of this is that the hedge species takes a number of years before it will flower again and subsequently bear fruit for wildlife and people. If the hedge is trimmed repeatedly at the same height, a 'hard knuckle' will start to form at that height – similar to the shape of a pollarded tree. Additionally, hedge trimming causes habitat destruction to species like the small eggar moth which spend nearly their entire life cycle in blackthorn and hawthorn hedgerow. This has led to a decline in the moth's population. It is now nationally scarce in Britain.

General Hedge Management

A 'hedgerow management' scale has been devised by an organisation called Hedgelink UK[15] ranging from 1 to 10. '1' describes the action to take for a heavily over trimmed hedge, '5' is a healthy dense hedgerow more than 2 metres in height, and '10' is a hedge that has not been managed at all and has become a line of trees. The RSPB suggest that hedges in Britain not be cut between March and August. This is to protect nesting birds, which are protected by law.

The techniques of coppicing and hard pollarding can be used to rejuvenate a hedge where hedge-laying is not appropriate.

Types of Hedges

Flowering evergreen and deciduous trees and shrubs can be used for hedges, especially where ornamental effect is a top priority, but where there may be insufficient room for border flowers. Plants with a naturally bushy habit are best for this purpose such as shrub roses, Berberis, Hebes and Escallonias.

Fedges are a cross between and hedge and a fence and are often used where space is too limited to accommodate the width of a hedge, or where a boundary is required to be erected straight away. The normal way to form a fedge is to grow a climbing plant such as Ivy, over a chicken wire or a chain link fence. Add timber posts to give the fedge a more formal appearance.

Mixed Hedges

Mixed Hedges consist of a variety of are made up of a variety of native species that in addition to providing screening also creates a refuge for different wildlife. Traditional mixed hedges might include Hawthorn, Hazel, Elderberry and Holly depending on local conditions.

Single Species Hedges

These are made up of a single species of a plant, such as Privet, Beech or Yew. They can be used as neutral backdrops for other more ornamental plants or simply used as to divide parts of the garden or enjoyed on their own.

Formal Hedges

These are indispensable in formal gardens not only for providing structure but for contributing to the overall tone of the space. The amount of formality afforded by the hedge depends upon the plant type and the frequency and style of pruning, with the most formal hedges being closely clipping Yew or Box or one of the smaller leaved conifers. Since Yew and Box respond so well to very close clipping, they are popular as subjects for topiary work.

Stilt Hedge

In this variation on the formal hedge, dense growth is carried high on straight parent trunks or stems. Used frequently in formal gardens in the past, they were often planted in double rows running parallel to each other.

Instant Hedge

The term instant hedge has become known since early this century for hedging plants that are planted collectively in such a way as to form a mature hedge from the moment they are planted together, with a height of at least 1.2 metres. They are usually created from hedging elements or individual plants which means very few are actually hedges from the start, as the plants need time to grow and entwine to form a real hedge.

An example of an instant hedge can be seen at the Elveden Hall Estate in East Anglia, where fields of hedges can be seen growing in cultivated rows, since 1998. The development of this type of mature hedge has led to such products being specified by landscape architects, garden designers, property developers, insurance companies, sports clubs, schools and local councils, as well as many private home owners. Demand has also increased from planning authorities in specifying to developers that mature hedges are planted rather than just whips (a slender, unbranched shoot or plant).

A 'real' instant hedge could be defined as having a managed root growth system allowing the hedge to be sold with a continuous rootstrips (rather than individual plants) which then enables year-round planting. During its circa 8-year production time, all stock should be irrigated, clipped and treated with controlled-release nutrients to optimise health.

Quickset Hedge

A quickset hedge is a type of hedge created by planting live whitethorn (common hawthorn) cuttings directly into the earth (hazel does not from cuttings). Once planted, these cuttings root and form new plants, creating a dense barrier. The technique is ancient, and the term quickset hedge is first recorded in 1484. The word quick in the name refers to the fact that the cuttings are living (as in "the quick and the dead"), and not to the speed at which the hedge grows, although it will establish quite rapidly. An alternative meaning of quickset hedging is any hedge formed of living plants or of living plants combined with a fence. The technique of quicksetting can also be used for many other shrubs and trees.

Devon Hedge

A Devon hedge is an earth bank topped with shrubs. The bank may be faced with turf or stone. When stone-faced, the stones are generally placed on edge, often laid flat around gateways.

A quarter of Devon's hedges are thought to be over 800 years old. There are approximately 33,000 miles (53,000 km) of Devon hedge, which is more than any other county. Traditional farming throughout the county has meant that fewer Devon hedges have been removed than elsewhere.

Devon hedges are particularly important for wildlife habitat. Around 20% of the UK's species-rich hedges occur within Devon. Over 600 species of flowering plants, 1500 species of insects, 65 species of birds and 20 species of mammals have been recorded living or feeding in Devon hedges. Hedge laying in Devon is usually referred to as steeping and involves cutting and laying steepers (the stems) along the top of the bank and securing them with crooks (forked sticks).

Cornish Hedge

A Cornish hedge is an earth bank with stones. It normally consists of large stone blocks constructed either side of a narrow earth bank, and held in place with interlocking stones. The neat rows of square stones at the top are called "edgers". The top of the hedge is planted with grass turf.

Sometimes hedging plants or trees are planted on the hedge to increase its windbreaking height. A rich flora develops over the lifespan of a Cornish hedge. The Cornish hedge contributes to the distinctive field-pattern of the Cornish landscape and its semi-natural wildlife habitat. There are about 30,000 miles (48,000 km) of hedges in Cornwall today.

Hedges suffer from the effects of tree roots, burrowing rabbits, rain, wind, farm animals and people. How often repairs are needed depends on how well the hedge was built, its stone, and what has happened to it since it was last repaired. Typically a hedge needs a cycle of repair every 150 years or so, or less often if it is fenced. Building new hedges, and repairing existing hedges, is a skilled craft, and there are professional hedgers in Cornwall.

You can decide to plant a hedge around your field, your smallholding or your urban garden (brick walls or fences with concrete posts don't have the benefits mentioned above). If you're serious, get a good book (the first one on that page is a good one) or attend a course. Search online for current grants for hedge planting and laying. Meanwhile here's some basic information for inspiration.

Types Of Plants For Edges

- Japanese Holly (Ilex crenata)

Japanese holly looks more like a boxwood shrub than holly shrub, bearing small, oval leaves. Many cultivars of this broadleaf evergreen are available. For hedge plants, most people select those that reach 3 to 4 feet in height with a similar spread.

- USDA Growing Zones: 5 to 8
- Color Varieties: White flowers
- Sun Exposure: Full to partial sun

- Soil Needs: Acidic soil that drains well

- English Holly (Ilex aquifolium)

English holly, with its prickly leaves, makes a better hedge plant than Japanese holly if you wish to combine security with aesthetic considerations. This is one type of holly that grows big enough to serve as a privacy screen (the 'Ferox Argentea' cultivar is 15 feet tall by 8 to 10 feet wide). Holly berries are toxic and should be kept away from children and pets.

- USDA Growing Zones: 5 to 9
- Color Varieties: Greenish-white flowers and red berries
- Sun Exposure: Full sun to partial shade
- Soil Needs: Well-drained, slightly acidic, fertile soil

- Barberry Bushes (Berberis thunbergii)

Sharp thorns line the barberry's branches, making it a traditional choice for security hedges. Its bright red berries persist through the cold-weather months to provide visual interest in winter. The thorns are present year-round. Until recently, barberry had fallen out of favor in North America due to its invasive nature. But the development of new, noninvasive cultivars may lead to a North American barberry revival.

- USDA Growing Zones: 4 to 8
- Color Varieties: Red berries; some varieties have purple foliage and yellow-orange flowers
- Sun Exposure: Full to partial sun
- Soil Needs: Well-drained soil

- Boxwood Shrubs (Buxus)

Boxwoods are the quintessential hedge plants. These broadleaf evergreens were adored by aristocratic Europeans for centuries as defining elements in formal garden design. North Americans living in deer country have found a new reason to love boxwood hedges: they are deer-resistant shrubs.

- USDA Growing Zones: 6 to 8
- Sun Exposure: Partial or dappled shade
- Soil Needs: Well-drained soil in the 6.8 to 7.5 pH range

- Mountain Laurels (Kalmia latifolia)

The mountain laurel is another broadleaf evergreen suitable for hedges. One of its best features is that it blooms in late spring to early summer. However, do not try to trim laurels as you would boxwoods. Laurels look best when they are allowed to grow into their natural mature shape. The pink-flowering types are the most popular.

- USDA Growing Zones: 4 to 9
- Color Varieties: Rose, pink, white; may have purple markings
- Sun Exposure: Partial shade to full sun
- Soil Needs: Cool, rich, moist, well-drained acidic soil

- Yew Bushes (Taxus)

Among needle-bearing evergreens, yew bushes are perhaps the most classic hedge plants. They are popular partly because they tolerate shade. While some yews grow tall enough to serve as privacy screens, yews are slow growers.

- USDA Growing Zones: 2 to 10, depending on the variety

- Color Varieties: Non-flowering; dark green needles and red berries
- Sun Exposure: Sun, partial shade, or full shade depending on variety
- Soil Needs: Well-draining soil with a neutral pH

- Lilacs (Syringa)

Deciduous hedge shrubs look great while in bloom but are just so-so during the winter. Also, because they drop their leaves and stand naked for part of the year, deciduous shrubs make for less-than-ideal privacy screens.

Lilac bushes are one of your more fragrant choices. To form a hedge with lilacs, simply plant several of them in a line, and do not fuss with making them conform to precise dimensions.

- USDA Growing Zones: 3 to 7
- Color Varieties: Lavender-blue, white, burgundy, deep purple, lilac
- Sun Exposure: Full sun
- Soil Needs: Loamy soil with neutral pH

- Rose of Sharon (Hibiscus syriacus)

Another deciduous shrub commonly found in hedges is the rose of Sharon. It is a valuable plant for gardeners wishing to maintain a continuous sequence of bloom because it is one of the late-summer flowering shrubs that display color during a part of the season when many other bushes have already finished blooming for the year.

- USDA Growing Zones: 5 to 9
- Color Varieties: White, red, lavender, or light blue
- Sun Exposure: Full sun to partial shade
- Soil Needs: Rich and moist

- Forsythia (Forsythia x intermedia)

Forsythia bushes are among the first plants to bloom in spring. You probably will not want to prune them as meticulously as you would, say, boxwood. Most people agree that these early-spring flowering shrubs look best when allowed to "have a bad hair day."

- USDA Growing Zones: 5 to 8
- Color Varieties: Yellow

- Sun Exposure: Full
- Soil Needs: Well-drained

- **Privet Hedges (Ligustrum)**

Like mountain laurels, privets are broadleaf shrubs that put out flowers, although their white flowers are not much of a selling point. However, not all varieties of privets are evergreen, and those that are will not necessarily grow well in your zone. Check with your local county extension to see if you can grow evergreen privets in your area. Also, ask if they are invasive in your region.

- USDA Growing Zones: 5 to 8
- Color Varieties: White flowers
- Sun Exposure: Full to partial sun
- Soil Needs: Tolerant of a variety of soil types

- **Azaleas (Rhododendron x Gable Stewartstonian)**

As with privets, azaleas can be either evergreen or deciduous, but their flowers are far superior to those on privets. Stewartstonian azalea has it all: Its dense branching structure makes it a good hedge plant (in contrast to the Exbury-type azalea, which has a looser branching structure). And, it is a shrub that blooms in early spring and offers good fall color. Azaleas also bear flowers in a range of colors, including red, pink, white, orange, and yellow.

- USDA Growing Zones: 5 to 8
- Color Varieties: Fertile, well-drained, and kept evenly moist
- Sun Exposure: Partial shade
- Soil Needs: Fertile, well-drained, acidic, and kept evenly moist

- Arborvitae (Thuja)

Arborvitae shrubs have a dense growth habit that makes them popular privacy screens or windbreaks. There are many types of arborvitae that come in various sizes, shapes, and colors. 'North Pole' and 'Emerald Green' are just about the right size for most hedge growers. 'Green Giant,' which can become 60 feet tall, is too big for small properties.

- USDA Growing Zones: 2 to 7
- Sun Exposure: Full to partial sun

- Soil Needs: Tolerates a range of soils but prefers moist well-drained loams

- Canadian Hemlocks (Tsuga canadensis)

Although Canadian hemlocks grow as trees in the wild, they are often sold in shrub form for use in hedges. The MacPhail Woods site states, "Prune hemlock lightly but often during the first few growing seasons (two to three times from late June to late August for two to three years). After three years, prune once, in late June, as with white spruce." The site cautions against cutting the leaders until the hemlock hedge or windbreak has attained the height you envisioned for it.

- USDA Growing Zones: 3 to 7
- Color Varieties: Small, yellow to light green
- Sun Exposure: Partial sun to partial shade
- Soil Needs: Rich, moist, acidic

Create private outdoor living spaces with a hedge. Determine the type of plant that best suits your needs; these top hedge picks make your choice easy.

- Boxwood

Boxwood sets the standard for formal clipped hedges. Its ability to withstand frequent shearing and shaping into perfect geometric forms makes this evergreen hedge plant a popular border plant. You can also let it grow tall to provide a screen or to create a maze. Some varieties grow to 20 feet tall.

- Name: Buxus selections
- Zones: 4–8

- Glossy Abelia

Butterflies love the trumpet-shape flowers that dangle from glossy abelias branches all summer long. This flowering hedge plant naturally forms an arching mound that grows 3 to 6 feet tall, but you can shear it to create a lower hedge.

- Name: Abelia x grandiflora
- Zones: 5–9

- Amur Maple

Grow hardy Amur maple as a small tree or large hedge and enjoy its spectacular red color in the fall. If you use it as a hedge, allow multiple trunks to grow, and shear their limbs occasionally to promote branching.

- Name: Acer ginnala
- Zones: 3–7

- Japanese Barberry

Barberry bears sharp spines that provide a nearly impenetrable barrier on this 3- to 6-foot-tall shrub. There's a wealth of varieties that bear foliage in shades of chartreuse, green, burgundy, and rosy red. The leaves develop golden, orange, and red hues in fall.

Test Garden Tip: In some areas, Japanese barberry is considered invasive, so check local regulations before planting.

- Name: Berberis selections

- Zones: 3–9

- Flowering Quince

Flowering quince is equipped with sharp spines that make it an effective barrier plant or privacy screen. The 6- to 10-foot-tall shrub lights up the early spring landscape with its scarlet, pink, or white blooms. Some varieties might rebloom in fall. The selection pictured here is 'Toyo Nishiki'.

- Name: Chaenomeles selections
- Zones: 4–8

- Sawara False Cypress

Sometimes called threadleaf false cypress for its delicate-looking foliage, this slow-growing evergreen hedge plant usually grows about 6 feet tall in 20 years, but eventually matures at 20 feet tall. Many cultivars with slight variations in foliage color and plant form are available.

- Name: Chamaecyparis pisifera
- Zones: 5–9

- Japanese Euonymus

This fast-growing hedge plant reaches 10–15 feet tall, but it's easy to shear it back to create a lower hedge. Create more landscape kick by selecting varieties of Japanese euonymus with gold-, cream-, or white-variegated foliage.

- Name: Euonymus japonicus
- Zones: 7–9

- Holly

If you prune them regularly, many species of holly work well as hedges. Dwarf hollies, such as dwarf yaupon holly, meserve holly, and inkberry, are the easiest types to use, as they need less pruning. Most varieties of holly bear red or orange berries, which are set off by the glossy evergreen foliage.

- Name: Ilex selections
- Zones: 3–10

- Juniper

Among the most versatile of evergreens, junipers range from ground-hugging creepers to mounded shrubs and upright trees. Whether you are looking for a steely blue groundcover or a tall tree for a fast-growing privacy hedge, junipers fit the bill. All respond well to pruning, making them useful hedges.

- Name: Juniperus selections
- Zones: 3–9

Other plants include:

Plants for a taller hedge 1.5m +

- Brachyglottis repanda
- Brachyglottis repanda 'Purpurea'
- Coprosma propinqua
- Coprosma repens
- Coprosma robusta
- Coprosma rugosa
- Corokia 'Bronze Knight
- Corokia buddlejioides
- Corokia cotoneaster
- Corokia 'Frosted Chocolate
- Corokia x. virgata 'Cheesemanii

- Dodonea viscosa
- Dodonaea viscosa 'Purpurea'
- Griselinia littoralis & cultivars
- Kunzea ericoides
- Leptospermum scoparium & cultivars
- Lophomyrtus bullata
- Lophomyrtus obcordata
- Lophomyrtus x ralphii & cultivars
- Metrosideros excelsa & cultivars
- Metrosideros kermadecensis 'Varigata'
- Metrosideros umbellata & cultivars
- Myrsine australis
- Nothofagus fusca
- Olearia cheesemanii
- Olearia 'Dartonii'
- Olearia macrodonta
- Olearia paniculata
- Olearia solandri
- Olearia traversii
- Pittosporum crassifolium
- Pittosporum eugenioides & cultivars
- Pittosporum ralphii
- Pittosporum tenuifolium & cutivars

- Plagiantus divaricatus (deciduous)
- Podocarpus acutifolius
- Podocarpus totara
- Podocarpus totara 'Aureus'

Plants for a hedge up to 1.5m

- Brachyglottis greyii
- Brachyglottis monroi
- Coprosma repens cultivars
- Corokia 'Geentys Green'
- Corokia 'Geentys Ghost'
- Corokia 'Silver Ghost'
- Corokia virgata
- Hebe albicans
- Hebe buchananii Hebe diosmifolia
- Hebe 'Emerald Gem'
- Hebe 'Inspiration'
- Hebe 'MacEwanii'
- Hebe odora
- Hebe pinguafolia
- Hebe pinguafolia var. sutherlandii
- Hebe recurva

- Hebe 'Red Edge'

- Hebe topiaria

- Hebe townsonii

- Hebe 'Wiri Cloud'

- Hebe 'Wiri Dawn'

- Hebe 'Wiri Mist'

- Hebe 'Wiri Splash'

- Olearia illicifolia x moschata Pittosporum' Pom Pom'

Steps For Planting Hedges

- Step 1: Plan Before Planting

Whether you're planting one hedge or many, planning is key. Decide where you want to plant. Will your hedges mark a property boundary? Border a front walkway or driveway? Frame a flower garden? You need to visualize the design and know exactly how much space you have to work with so you can space plants appropriately for well-designed, interlocking growth.

If you're not sure what kind of hedges you want to plant, do some research on the Internet or consult gardening publications to find out which type will work best in your soil, in your region, and meet the intended application. For our purposes here, there are two basic categories of hedge plants: evergreen and deciduous. Of these, evergreens are the most common, and the type that usually comes to mind when one thinks of hedges. When buying hedge plants, be sure you know how they grow and how much they grow, especially if you'll be intermixing different types of shrubs for your hedgerow.

Deciduous plants lose their leaves in winter. If you want year-round hedges, plant evergreen hedge plants. Visit your local nursery to buy plants and to get help if you are unsure which plants best suit your needs. Nurseries will have the plants prepared with their root balls snuggly wrapped in a layer of burlap to keep them safe and ready for when you take them home to plant. To estimate how many plants to buy and the appropriate spacing between each one, measure the length of your hedge site. Generally, for common boxwood hedge plants, 2' to 3' between each plant is adequate. Ask a nursery employee for help with deciding how many plants to purchase and how much space should be between each plant. Larger, taller plants for a privacy hedge can require 6' or more between each plant.

Note: Try to choose plants that are at or close to the height that you want your hedge to be. Keep in mind though, that larger plants may require some additional hands to help you move them around. Ask a family member, a friend or a neighbor to be your assistant.

To avoid damage, always pick up your shrubs by the root ball and not the trunk.

- Step 2: Prepare Planting Site

Use a tape measure to determine the dimensions of your planting site. The length will vary; width is what you want to pay special attention to. The width can vary also, due to the size of plants. A good rule of thumb is that the site should be about 1' wider than the root ball. So, measure out a width of 2' to 3' for a standard-sized hedge. Using a hammer, drive wooden stakes into the ground to mark this measurement. Continue hammering stakes at this width in intervals along the required length of the site. Attach a length of gardening twine to one stake by tying it and then run the twine along the rest of the stakes in the same way to mark your hedge site.

Add a 2" layer of compost or organic fertilizer (according to directions) to the planting site and then use a tiller to break up the soil and mix it and compost/fertilizer together. Lightly water the site using a garden hose.

- Step 3: Dig a Trench

Use a shovel to dig a trench inside your staked-off site, along the length of the site. Trench depth will vary, but make sure the hole is slightly less deep than the root ball is high. It should be deep enough so that root balls are below ground level with about 1" of the plant left above ground. Measure one of the plants' root balls before digging. Generally, depth probably will be around 1'.

Safety Alert: It's a good idea to check with your local utility companies about the location of gas, water, telephone or other utility lines and if there are any digging restrictions or requirements for those areas.

Note: Save yourself considerable cleanup time by piling the soil that was removed for the trench onto a plastic sheet or tarp. This also prevents the piled dirt from damaging the grass around the trench.

- Step 4: Plant Hedge

Stamp down the soil in the bottom of the trench with your foot so it is firm and won't sink after your hedge plants have been planted. Place each plant into the trench. Check to see that the top of the root balls are at or a little higher than ground level. Use a utility knife to cut any twine wrapped around trunks and fold down the burlap around the sides of each root ball. Don't remove the burlap completely as this can damage the root balls. The plants' roots will grow through the burlap into the surrounding soil and the burlap will eventually deteriorate.

Fill in the trench around the sides of each root ball and pat it around the ball firmly. Form a mound of soil around the bottom of the tree that will allow water to pool there like a basin. This will help keep the roots well-watered until the shrubs are established. Add 2" to 3" of mulch to combat weeds, retain moisture and insulate your hedge from temperature extremes. Be careful not to cover the trunk; keep a 1" to 2" "no-mulch" ring around it.

Note : It's a good idea to mix some peat moss and a small amount of plant food into the soil you replace around your new hedge. After planting, use pruning shears to cut off any dead or damaged growth and remove any wayward branches that don't conform to the shape of your hedge. Water the planting site thoroughly so that the roots can become established.

- Step 5: Maintain Hedge

Prune hedges regularly to promote health, growth and density. Once per month during growing season should be adequate. This will keep the plant at peak growth and shape your hedge so that it looks its best. Cut just a couple of inches off at a time so you're cutting into newest growth. Remove dead or diseased branches. Wrap up pruning about a month before it gets cold in your region, as new growth will be exposed to cold temperatures which can harm the plant.

Note: Keep the hedge shape uniform. If the top of the hedge becomes wider than the bottom, it will shade the bottom of the plant and weaken it. Water the hedge regularly to keep it healthy and productive. Add fertilizer to the soil at least once a year during the growing season.

What Are The Benefits Of Hedges?

These days, it's much cheaper and easier for a farmer to install a wire fence than to plant and manage a hedge. There are grants to encourage hedge planting and laying, but there are also plenty of benefits for smallholders really, rather than industrial farms.

Hedges provide numerous benefits to livestock, including, previously, protection from large predators (bears existed in the UK until the early Middle Ages, and wolves until the 15th century in England and maybe 300 years later in Scotland) especially the youngsters. They also provide windbreaks, plus additions to their diet – animals love to nibble on hedges. They help stop the spread of diseases in animals, as they can't touch each other through a hedge, as they can with a fence. Hedges provide food for humans too – blackberries, sloes, hazelnuts, hops, rose hips etc.

Hedges are a boon for wildlife, such as hedgehogs, insects, amphibians, birds, voles and shrews, snakes, lizards etc., providing food, shelter, blossom for pollinators, and corridors for movement.

They also store carbon and prevent soil erosion. In cities, hedges are good at combatting pollution. They're better than trees for absorbing particulates, as their leaves are at exhaust level, rather than up in the canopy. The privet around urban gardens is a cultivar bred from the native privet, which is also used in hedging. They also add beauty to the landscape (at least something good came out of the horror of the enclosures).

- They can add green structure

They may take a lot more time and maintenance than built fences and walls, but hedges create a soft, tranquil atmosphere that only living, green walls can provide. In winter, when gardens tend to look bare, an evergreen hedge creates a year round structured look. In contemporary gardens they can be used to reinforce the architectural lines of the house, to give a crisp defined look as shown in this stunner by well-known designer Peter Fudge.

- They can frame views and define paths

Clipped hedges are one of the best devices to direct the eye through the garden to a particular view or vista. They can be used to frame a view as well. In this formal Melbourne garden, they not only create a vista, they also define the paths and beds, adding a sense of unity to the garden.

- The can disguise untidy areas

We all know hedges are ideal for screening neighbours and hiding unsightly views such as ugly fences or sheds. But consider also using them as a low edge to disguise bedraggled or weedy garden beds and stop birds from digging up your soil. They're also an effective noise barrier for traffic, trains and neighbours – the denser the hedge, the better it will reduce noise. Evergreen species are best for year round noise control.

- They can provide colour and interest

If you choose the right species, you can use hedges to add extra interest to the garden. For a romantic, soft look, use flowering hedge cultivars of lavender (pictured), Camellia, Michelia, Hebe and rosemary. Hedges with coloured foliage such as Photinia, Teucrium and barberry (Berberis) are often used to make a bold statement in contemporary gardens. For winter interest, consider hedge species that produce berries such as cultivars of Viburnum, Indian Hawthorn (Rhaphiolepis umbellata) and Eugenia.

- They can extend your plant palette

Rather than commonly used box hedges, why not vary your plant selections and go for more contemporary hedging plants such as fig (Ficus) species, hebes, dwarf bottlebrush (Callistemon 'Little John'), Chilean guava (Myrtus ugni), dwarf camellias or Japanese holly (Ilex crenata)?

- They can be cheap to grow

You need a lot of plants for a hedge and that can be expensive. Buying small plants will save you money and they will adapt better to the conditions in your garden than larger specimens that have been grown in the optimum conditions of a nursery. Often they will reach the same height as larger and more expensive plants quite quickly anyway. Some nurseries will discount if you buy in bulk. Another cost saving method of growing a hedge is to take cuttings. Try Buxus and Teucrium as these grow easily from cuttings.

- They are easy to plant

Wait until late autumn or winter when the ground is moist before planting new hedges. This allows their root systems to become well established before the soil starts to dry out. Water new plants every day for at least a month if the weather stays dry. Make sure you don't plant trees close to drainage or sewerage pipes as their roots can cause major damage. Add lots of compost, organic matter and slow release fertiliser to the soil before planting, particularly if it is heavy clay (or consider raised beds if drainage is really bad). Be generous when digging planting holes. These must be the same depth as the root ball of the tree or shrub and at least twice as wide. Use a string line and pegs to mark planting positions.

- The are better trimmed early

Start shaping your hedge when plants are very young to keep growth dense and even. It should be wider at the bottom with slightly sloping sides to allow light onto the lower leaves. New hedges planted last winter or autumn can be cut back hard late spring or early summer, then trimmed lightly again in late summer.

- They can create screening where you need it

One of the most common mistakes people make in gardens is to plant trees for screening then leave them untrimmed. As the trees grow taller, most of their foliage will grow on the top branches where the light is, while the lower branches remain bare. This of course means lots of gaps right where you don't want them. By trimming the top and sides of tall screen trees to around a metre above fence height (also known as pleaching or hedges on stilts), you'll get screening where you need it, without blocking light from coming into your garden. It also creates a neater, more architectural look.

- They perform best when looked after properly

Keeping an eye on the basics will make a big difference to the look of your hedge. With regular feeding and watering, you will get more lush growth and healthier plants that can fight off pests and diseases. There's nothing worse than spending several years nurturing a lovely hedge, then losing one or two plants – sadly, a common problem with hedges.

Conclusion

Growing a hedge is not as hard, many of us think "I don't know how to, so I doubt I would be able to grow one", but it's easy, just make sure you choose the right plant. Seek good garden advice from our staff on what you want to achieve, what plants would be suitable in your area. Hedges can be used to divide up areas of your garden, just like walls in a house. Hedges add a different dimension to the garden that can never be matched by any type of constructed fence. It's a living garden feature that will attract birds, change colour with the seasons and it height adjustable. I don't know of any fence that you can cut back, and the next year you can let it grow a little taller if you like.